HIP-HOP
ARTISTS

KENDRICK LAMAR

RAP **TITAN**

BY SARAH ASWELL

Essential Library

An Imprint of Abdo Publishing
abdopublishing.com

ABDOPUBLISHING.COM

Published by Abdo Publishing, a division of ABDO, PO Box 398166, Minneapolis, Minnesota 55439. Copyright © 2018 by Abdo Consulting Group, Inc. International copyrights reserved in all countries. No part of this book may be reproduced in any form without written permission from the publisher. Essential Library™ is a trademark and logo of Abdo Publishing.

Printed in the United States of America, North Mankato, Minnesota
102017
012018

Cover Photo: Amy Harris/Invision/AP Images
Interior Photos: Danny Payne/Rex Features/AP Images, 4; Kathy Hutchins/Shutterstock Images, 9, 13, 51; Matt Sayles/Invision/AP Images, 11, 74–75, 86, 97; John Salangsang/Invision/AP Images, 14; Christian Bertrand/AP Images, 16, 82; Paul Sakuma/AP Images, 19; Kathy Kmonicek/AP Images, 22; Shutterstock Images, 24, 43, 81; Frank Wiese/AP Images, 28; Seth Poppel/Yearbook Library, 31; Chelsea Lauren/Rex Features/AP Images, 33; Matt Sayles/AP Images, 36; Everett Collection/Shutterstock Images, 39; Jerry Perez/PacificCoastNews/Newscom, 41; Abel Fermin/Rex Features/AP Images, 47; Dana Nalbandian/WireImage/Getty Images, 48; Robert E. Klein/AP Images, 52–53; David Goldman/AP Images, 57; John Amis/Invision/AP Images, 58–59; Roger Kisby/Getty Images Entertainment/Getty Images, 60; Joe Seer/Shutterstock Images, 65; Kobby Dagan/Shutterstock Images, 68; Christian Bertrand/Shutterstock Images, 70–71; Jeff Lombardo/Invision/AP Images, 78; RMV/Rex Features/AP Images, 85; Bennett Raglin/Getty Images Entertainment/Getty Images, 88; Johnny Nunez/Getty Images Entertainment/Getty Images, 90–91; Amy Harris/Invision/AP Images, 92–93; Larry Busacca/Getty Images Entertainment/Getty Images, 95

Editor: Brenda Haugen
Series Designer: Laura Polzin

PUBLISHER'S CATALOGING-IN-PUBLICATION DATA

Names: Aswell, Sarah, author.
Title: Kendrick Lamar: rap titan / by Sarah Aswell.
Other titles: Rap titan
Description: Minneapolis, Minnesota : Abdo Publishing, 2018. | Series: Hip-hop
    artists | Includes online resources and index.
Identifiers: LCCN 2017946866 | ISBN 9781532113291 (lib.bdg.) | ISBN 9781532152177
    (ebook)
Subjects: LCSH: Kendrick Lamar (Kendrick Duckworth), 1987-.—Juvenile literature.
    | Rap musicians— United States—Biography—Juvenile literature. | Rap
    (Music)—Juvenile literature.
Classification: DDC 782.421649 [B]—dc23
LC record available at https://lccn.loc.gov/2017946866

CONTENTS

THE ANTHEM OF A GENERATION

Hundreds of activists from around the country gathered in Cleveland, Ohio, for the Movement for Black Lives conference in July 2015. The activists were part of the Black Lives Matter movement, which fights to end racism and violence against African Americans in the United States. On the last day of the conference, people attending the event protested in the streets near Cleveland State University. As the crowd filled the street, they chanted, "We gon' be alright! We gon' be alright! We gon' be alright!"[1] Video of the people chanting was seen around the world, and soon people at other Black Lives Matter marches and protests were chanting the same phrase.

The chant was the hook from Kendrick Lamar's song "Alright." The song is about many of the issues that are important to the Black Lives Matter movement, such as fighting racism, police brutality, and inequality. But even

Lamar's music provides hope while still tackling difficult subjects.

5

though the song is about serious subjects, it has an energetic, hopeful, and uplifting tone.

"The chorus [of 'Alright'] is simple yet extraordinarily intoxicating, easy to chant, offering a kind of comfort that people of color and other oppressed communities desperately need all too often: the hope—the *feeling*—that despite tensions in this country growing worse and worse, in the long run, we're all gon' be all right."[2]

—Aisha Harris, Slate.com, August 3, 2015

As more protests used the hook as a chant, people started calling "Alright" a protest song. Others said it was a civil rights anthem. Some even called it the new black national anthem.

WRITING "ALRIGHT"

Kendrick Lamar was traveling around the country in 2014 and recording his third full-length album, *To Pimp a Butterfly*. His friend and fellow rapper Pharrell Williams created a beat for the album. He asked Lamar to write rap lyrics to go with it.

Lamar loved the beat, which was strong but positive. It sounded jazzy, fun, and smooth, and Williams knew it was special. Lamar thought it was special too, but he did not know what lyrics to write to go with the song.

Next, Williams wrote the hook for the song: "We gon' be alright!" At that point, Lamar knew they were creating more than a song. It was a statement. It was a protest song. But he still did not know the right words to accompany the music and hook. He wanted the song to be great, but that made it even harder to put his thoughts on paper.

For six months, Williams encouraged Lamar to write the words to the song, but Lamar was stuck. Finally, one day the lyrics came to Lamar. He was thinking about how he had traveled to South Africa and observed how black people there were struggling even harder against racism and oppression than Americans were. He realized he could either rise up and fight, or he could fall

THE BLACK LIVES MATTER MOVEMENT

The Black Lives Matter movement began in 2013, after a man named George Zimmerman was found not guilty of shooting and killing an unarmed 17-year-old African-American named Trayvon Martin in Florida. Some people believe Trayvon was killed—and Zimmerman was set free—because of racism.

The movement grew as more people became aware of how African Americans are often treated unfairly by police officers and in court. Across the country, Black Lives Matter marches and protests happened each time an incidence of police brutality was reported. At the same time, the #BlackLivesMatter hashtag was used to unite and educate people online.

WHAT IS A PROTEST SONG?

A protest song makes a political statement or is part of a social movement. Protest songs have been around for centuries in the United States and often become more popular in times of war or political conflict. Protest songs were very popular in the 1960s, when many folk and rock musicians sang tunes that were pro–civil rights and antiwar. Today, a new era of protest songs has emerged with the Black Lives Matter movement. Most of these new protest songs are written and performed by rap and hip-hop artists.

victim to the situation. He quickly scribbled down all the words.

He texted the lyrics to Williams, who answered that he knew they were the right words for the song. "Alright" was born. The song is about a lot of things. It is about slavery and the history of African Americans in the United States. It is about civil rights. It is about racism and police violence. Most of all, it is about overcoming problems and staying positive. It is about being proud and having courage.

RELEASING THE SINGLE

"Alright" was released as a single in the summer of 2015. While it did not rise to the top of the charts, it had a huge impact. The song won two Grammy Awards in 2016, for

2015 BET AWARDS PERFORMANCE

Weeks before the Cleveland protest, Lamar performed "Alright" at the beginning of the 2015 Black Entertainment Television (BET) Awards in Los Angeles, California. Lamar rapped the song from on top of a graffiti-covered police car, while a giant, slightly tattered American flag waved behind him. As the song peaked, dancers with flags marched to fill the stage and aisles, symbolizing a protest. The performance was a stand against police brutality and a positive statement about the future. Later that night, Lamar won a BET Award for Best Male Hip Hop Artist.

Best Rap Performance and Best Rap Song. It was also nominated for two other Grammys—Best Music Video and Song of the Year. Many magazines and music critics put "Alright" at the top of their list of the best songs of the year. But most important, it became a protest song and anthem for many people fighting injustice. It made people think and feel.

CHANGING HISTORY

Today, Kendrick Lamar is considered one of the top rap artists performing. He is also considered one of the most influential artists in the world. His music inspires other artists as well as his fans because it has strong messages and imagery.

Lamar's music has earned him critical acclaim and many awards.

LAMAR'S CREATIVE PROCESS

Since he was in elementary school, Lamar has been bursting with creative ideas and stories. Today, he says he is still constantly thinking about music and lyrics. He has said that his creative process is half freestyle rapping in the studio and half writing his ideas down. He likes to write lots of ideas and verses onto scraps of paper and then piece them all together into a song.

Lamar writes every day, even when he is on tour. He told *XXL* magazine, "I can't miss a day without writing, whether it's a line, a verse, or an idea. I always have to have that creative flow going."[3]

Lamar combines many styles of music into his rap, including R&B, jazz, and rock and roll. His beats are energetic and poppy, and his lyrics are often very meaningful. Songs such as "Alright" get listeners to dance and also to think.

Rap and hip-hop music have a long history of rebelling against authority and exploring racism. Lamar's music has brought that tradition to the next level. He writes powerful protest music for the next generation, which not only talks openly about society's problems but also how people can unite and solve them.

COMING UP IN COMPTON

Kendrick Lamar Duckworth was born in Compton, California, on June 17, 1987. He has three younger siblings, though he was an only child for the first seven years of his life.

His parents, Paula Oliver and Kenny Duckworth, moved to Compton from Chicago, Illinois, when they were teenagers. Kenny was escaping gang involvement, and the couple wanted a fresh start. They did not know that Compton also had gang violence.

Paula and Kenny packed their clothes into trash bags, took a train to Compton, and started their new life with just $500. Paula got a job at McDonald's and did hair for $20 a head, while Kenny worked at Kentucky Fried Chicken (KFC). The couple slept in motels, cars, and parks until they saved enough money for an apartment. Three years after they moved to Compton, Kendrick was born.

Lamar attends the premier of the 2015 movie *Straight Outta Compton*.

COMPTON AND THE LOS ANGELES RIOTS

Compton is a city near Los Angeles in southern California. Growing up in Compton in the 1980s and 1990s was difficult. At the time, the city was mostly black, and racism and police brutality toward African Americans were common. Poverty, crime, drugs, and gang violence were not unusual either. In 1990, the city had a very high murder rate of 91 homicides per 100,000 residents.[1]

Though Kendrick doesn't worry about money anymore, his music is influenced by the poverty of his youth.

Kendrick experienced poverty early in his life. His parents both worked in fast food restaurants, but they often required welfare and food stamps to afford food, clothing, and shelter. Kendrick remembers walking with his mother to get food stamps from a government building. Kendrick has said that his dad was also involved in crime to help the family get by. Because of all the poverty in Compton, criminal activity was common. Kendrick and his father have not talked about the crimes Kenny committed. Kendrick says that his parents wanted to keep him innocent. His father told *Rolling Stone*, "I don't want to talk about that bad time. But I did what I had to do."[2]

"People make a big thing about Compton, and growing up I heard all kind of things about the place I was raised, but when you live in it, it becomes normal. . . . If you grow up only watching people in gangs, you won't see anything different unless someone shows you something to break that cycle. Music can show someone something positive."[3]

–Kendrick Lamar

Kendrick was also exposed to violence at a young age. When he was just five years old, he saw his first murder when a drug dealer was shot outside of his apartment. At eight years old, Kendrick saw his second murder when a man was shot in a car while ordering food at a popular neighborhood hamburger stand. Later, Kendrick talked about seeing such traumatic events at a young age: "You just get numb to it."[4]

When Kendrick was four years old, riots took place in Los Angeles. He remembers smoke from fires, running crowds, and his father stealing car tires. Kendrick also remembers his family members talking about stealing during the riots. Only later, when he watched television, did he understand that the riots were about a black man being beaten by white police officers.

The 1992 LA riots were the first time that Kendrick was exposed to the issue of police brutality. It was also the first time he saw the anger about police brutality and

A fire burns out of control during the 1992 LA riots.

racism in the black community. Years later, he would sing about police brutality in the present day and help other people understand.

KENDRICK AS A KID

Even though growing up in poverty and around crime was difficult, Kendrick had a happy childhood. His mother and father loved him. Kendrick said that he never knew his parents experienced hard times financially because they always managed to get him a present for Christmas and his birthday.

Kendrick and his three siblings grew up in a small, three-bedroom house that was painted blue. His parents received government assistance to pay rent for Section 8 housing in a high-crime area.

Kendrick's happy life mixed with the violence around him. Kendrick loved to ride his bike, listen to music, and eat at Tam's Burgers, a local restaurant that was right down the street. It was also where Lamar saw his first murder.

MUSICAL INFLUENCES

Kendrick Lamar remembers house parties with his parents, aunts, uncles, and his many cousins. The adults would play a mix of oldies and early 1990s West Coast rap, including Eazy-E, Too Short, E-40, Marvin Gaye, and the Isley Brothers. Kendrick was named after one of the members of the Temptations, Eddie Kendricks.

Kendrick also listened to jazz and funk musicians, such as John Coltrane, Miles Davis, and George Clinton and Parliament Funkadelic. These sounds would come alive again in Kendrick's later studio albums. His favorite rappers include Jay-Z, Nas, Tupac, Snoop Dogg, Notorious B.I.G., and Eminem.

Kendrick remembers doing back flips off of his friends' roofs, but he also recalls the sounds of sirens and gunfire.

Kendrick remembers playing with his cousins at his family's house parties. The group would get in trouble for riding Big Wheels in the house, but they also listened to the adults' music—oldies and gangsta rap.

During the summer, Kendrick loved to go to Lueders Park to swim. It was a 30-minute walk and an even shorter bike ride from his home. One summer, the mayor of Compton paid the fees so kids could swim for free, and Kendrick went every day.

KENDRICK AND HIS DAD

Every weekend, Kenny took Kendrick to the Compton Swap Meet, a place with lots of little stores. The pair would buy cassette tapes and CDs by local rappers at the Cycadelic Music Corner. Kenny also bought Kendrick Nike sneakers for school. Sometimes they would see a famous rapper at the

WHAT IS GANGSTA RAP?

Gangsta rap became popular just after Kendrick Lamar was born, when the rap group N.W.A. released *Straight Outta Compton* in 1988. The music is tough, edgy, and profane. In the beginning, gangsta rap was created by artists who were part of gangs or who were former members. The lyrics were often about gang life, including poverty, crime, and violence. Often, the songs glorified gang life, shootings, and drug dealing. Later, many gangsta rap artists were not in gangs but wrote fictionalized stories about gang life. Gangsta rap is also often about ego, money, strength, and status.

Although Kendrick grew up in Compton and was influenced by gangsta rap, he is not a gangsta rapper. He raps about his life growing up around gangs, but he does not glorify it. He thinks music can help people in Compton see there are options besides gang involvement. He also tries to be humble.

Growing up in an area where gun violence was a common problem shaped Kendrick's worldview and musical perspective.

Compton Swap Meet. They even saw music executive Suge Knight there.

Similar to many young men in Compton, Kenny was involved in gang activity and crime. He felt like he did it to help his family with money. It also was part of the culture in Compton. For example, two of Lamar's uncles, who also moved from Chicago to Compton, went to jail for a long time for robbery. A third uncle was murdered during gang violence. Although Kendrick's father was involved in the gang lifestyle, he was always there for his son. Kendrick has said that his father's love, attention, and guidance are the reasons he did not become involved in gangs.

FAMOUS RAPPERS FROM COMPTON

Kendrick was not the first famous rapper to grow up in Compton. In fact, a large number of West Coast rappers hail from that city.

Easy-E, Ice Cube, and Dr. Dre were all raised in Compton in the 1960s and 1970s. In the late 1980s, they formed the group N.W.A. and rocketed to fame after the release of their debut studio album, *Straight Outta Compton*. Their powerful, controversial music dealt with issues such as gang activity and police violence.

Jayceon Terrell Taylor, whose stage name is The Game, or simply Game, was born in Compton in 1979 into a rough life. He endured poverty, crime, and violence. He was placed in foster care at seven years old. Approximately six years later, one of his older brothers was murdered in gang violence. After being involved in gangs and drugs, The Game was shot. He decided to turn his life around and began rapping. He was soon discovered by Dr. Dre and Aftermath records.

DISCOVERING POETRY AND RAP

In many ways, Kendrick was like other kids in his neighborhood. He was poor but had a happy childhood. He was often in the midst of crime and violence. He dreamed of being a basketball star or rapper. But as he grew older, people started to notice he was different. He was reserved and observant. He loved telling stories. He did well in school.

During junior high school and high school, Kendrick discovered his passions. However, he also made some bad choices, which almost led him down the wrong path.

A QUIET KID WHO STUTTERED

Kendrick's family and friends recall that he was a loner as a boy and was not outspoken. He would rather listen and observe the room than participate in the action.

Kendrick found his voice onstage.

UNDERSTANDING STUTTERING

Stuttering or stammering is a speech disorder that makes it more difficult to communicate. Stuttering is when a person repeats parts of words, prolongs sounds, or suddenly stops between sounds or words. Approximately 1 percent of people stutter, including 5 percent of young children.[1] Most children who stutter grow out of it either naturally or with the help of speech therapy.

Stuttering is mostly genetic. Research shows stuttering may develop because a person's brain processes speech differently. It can be treated in both children and adults with speech therapy. Kendrick Lamar is not the only famous musician with a history of stuttering. Other famous musical stutterers include Marc Anthony, Nicole Kidman, Marilyn Monroe, Elvis Presley, Ed Sheeran, and Noel Gallagher.

One of the reasons Kendrick did not talk much was that, until middle school, he had a noticeable stutter. He stumbled on certain words but only when he was excited or in trouble. The stutter made him think he could never be a rapper. Instead, he wanted to be a professional basketball player.

It turned out later that his stuttering did not hurt his music. It actually helped. He has said that he put his energy into making music when he was a kid because it was a way for him to get his thoughts out smoothly. His stuttering went away when he was rapping and finally faded as he grew up.

CALIFORNIA LOVE

On one of Kendrick's weekend adventures with his dad, the pair went to the Compton Swap Meet as usual. But unlike most weekends, the street was blocked off and a crowd was gathered. Eight-year-old Kendrick sat on his father's shoulders to see what was happening.

Kendrick saw rap legends Dr. Dre and Tupac Shakur shooting their music video for a remix of "California Love." The song would later become one of the most famous rap songs of the era. In the video, the two rappers celebrate their home state while dancing with friends and riding in a black Bentley.

Kendrick was impressed with more than the famous rappers' lifestyles. At one point, a police officer on

DR. DRE, TUPAC, AND "CALIFORNIA LOVE"

In 1995, rapper Tupac Shakur was released from prison and signed a new contract with Death Row Records. He was eager to start recording songs right away. According to producer and DJ Chris Taylor, Tupac showed up at a barbecue at Dr. Dre's house after being released from prison. Dre had just finished creating the beat for "California Love." Tupac jumped into the recording booth and added his bars in just 20 minutes.

The single, a sunny party song about southern California, spent two weeks at Number 1 on the *Billboard* 100. It was also nominated for two Grammy Awards in 1997—Best Rap Solo Performance and Best Rap Performance by a Duo or Group.

Tupac was shot and died in September 1996. His murder remains unsolved.

a motorcycle who was controlling traffic almost scraped the Bentley. In response, Tupac yelled at the officer to be careful. Kendrick was amazed that Tupac stood up to the officer without being afraid of police retaliation.

AN INSPIRATIONAL TEACHER

Like many top musicians, Kendrick was inspired by one of his teachers. When Kendrick entered seventh grade, an English teacher named Regis Inge taught the class about poetry. A whole new world opened up for Kendrick. He loved learning about poetry techniques, such as alliteration, rhyming, and metaphors.

Inge recognized Kendrick's talent for expressing himself. Kendrick recalls that after he rushed to complete his first poetry assignment for the class, he was surprised he earned an A. His friends got Cs and Ds. Kendrick realized his teacher saw he was special.

Kendrick started writing at home, at first for class and then for himself. His parents thought he was just doing homework. "You could put all your feelings down on a sheet of paper, and they'd make sense to you," Kendrick said. "I liked that."[2]

Inge continued to encourage and guide Kendrick after he left middle school. The two still play basketball when Kendrick visits home.

RAP AND POETRY DEVICES

Many tools and techniques used in poetry are also used in Kendrick's verses. Some include:

Alliteration: The repetition of a sound during a phrase or sentence that adds interest and rhythm to the words.

Double entendre: A word or phrase that has two meanings, one of which is usually funny, dark, or even offensive.

Imagery: Using language to create a sensory experience that involves sight, touch, smell, taste, and sound.

Metaphor: A comparison between two unlikely objects, ideas, or feelings.

Repetition: The repeated use of a word or phrase in order to stress its importance or create a feeling.

Symbolism: Using a word or object to represent a greater idea, object, or feeling.

RAPPER POET

Kendrick never forgot the poetry lessons he learned in Regis Inge's English class. Today, fans, critics, and musicians often discuss the literary bent of Lamar's music and lyrics. Pharrell Williams compared Kendrick to folk singer Bob Dylan, another musician with poetic lyrics, who won the Pulitzer Prize for literature in 2016.

Adam Bradley, a professor who studies the poetry of pop music, has pointed out Kendrick's storytelling skills as well as his use of poetry techniques. For example, when he rhymes "win again" and "Wimbledon" in his song "DNA," Kendrick is using a mosaic rhyme, rhyming a phrase with a word that has more than one syllable.[3]

RUNNING WITH THE WRONG CROWD

Kendrick was doing well in school and had two loving, attentive parents. But Kendrick recalls being involved in fights and small crimes, such as trespassing and theft. Kendrick also experimented with alcohol and drugs during this time.

In high school, Kendrick's mother once found him crying in the front yard because someone had shot at him. Another time, police delivered Kendrick to his front door because he was involved in an illegal incident in the neighborhood. His parents kicked him out of the house for two days.

Kendrick's father was also involved in gang activity and crime, but Kenny disapproved of his son following in his footsteps. Kendrick told *Spin Magazine* that Kenny sat

him down when he was 16 years old: "My father said, 'I don't want you to be like me.' I said, '*What you mean you don't want me to be like you?*' I couldn't really grasp the concept."[4]

> "My family seen I had a fond passion for certain things, and I was real intricate with the detail, watching and studying. Even though I was surrounded by all this [gang] stuff, it wasn't in my nature. Music became my outlet, and I ran with it."[5]
>
> –*Kendrick Lamar*

Kendrick did not listen to Kenny at first. Kenny warned Kendrick not to get into a car with boys who were up to mischief. Kendrick got into the car anyway. Later, after Kendrick got into trouble with the boys for trying to steal from a house, Kendrick realized Kenny was right. "What separated me from my friends getting locked up, going to jail for life, or being dead in prison was the fact that after I bumped my head, [my dad] was always there to say, 'I told you,'" Kendrick said in an interview with the website *Rap Dose* in 2011. "I was just blessed, man, you know? And my pops, he wasn't perfect, I mean, he was a street dude. But he always had that wisdom and that knowledge to say, "I've been there, I've done that. Don't do that.'"[6]

Kenny told Kendrick, "Things I have done, mistakes I've made, I never want you to make those mistakes. You can wind up out on the corner."[7] Kendrick knew his dad noticed that he was not keeping good company. Out of respect for his father, Kendrick changed his ways, but not before he got into trouble several times for breaking the law.

RUN-INS WITH THE POLICE

Kendrick never got deeply involved in crime or gang violence, but he still had several interactions with the police when he was a teen. When he was 17, he was in the passenger seat of his friend Moose's car when they were pulled over. Moose could not get his drivers license out fast enough, and the officer suddenly pulled a gun. Kendrick and Moose were let go without incident, but Kendrick was so angry and shaken by the incident that he cried.

Another time, Kendrick and his friends were breaking the law when a police officer caught them. The kids ran, and the officer pulled a gun. "We was in the wrong," Kendrick said in an interview with *Rolling Stone* without giving details about what they were doing. "But we just kids. It's not worth pulling your gun out over. Especially when we running away."[8] No one was hurt, but it left an impact on Kendrick.

These police interactions made Kendrick think about the role of law enforcement as well as the issues of police brutality and racism. He saw both sides of the story. He knew it was wrong to break the law, but he also knew it was wrong for police officers to treat others unfairly.

STILL RESERVED

Even with his stutter now gone, Kendrick is still quiet and reflective. He describes himself as an introvert and observer. Unlike many rappers and superstars, he would rather create songs in his studio than show up at parties or clubs. He has a circle of close friends and family. Many people in his social circle today are people he has known since childhood. His emotions and strong opinions all come out through his music and performances.

Although this time of his life was dark and dangerous, Kendrick learned a lot about himself. He recognized his love for words and writing and his need to express his feelings. He also learned a lot about his culture and the problems facing his city and the United States. He would rap about all of these lessons for years to come.

MAKING MIXTAPES AND MORE

Today, Kendrick Lamar performs in front of thousands of people and is considered one of the best rappers in the world. He makes strong statements about political and social issues. His songs can be loud, fierce, and fiery. But outside of music, he is a quiet, introverted person who does not like to be the center of attention. How did such a quiet person break into the rap scene?

RAPPING AFTER SCHOOL

As his interest in poetry and storytelling grew, Kendrick began rapping in middle school. He wrote rhymes and rapped at school with friends starting at age 13. When he was at Centennial High School, he entered the freestyle

Away from music, Kendrick tends to be a quiet person.

50 Cent was one of Kendrick's earliest business influences.

WHAT IS FREESTYLE BATTLE RAP?

Kendrick participated in freestyle rap battles while in high school. During a rap battle, two artists take turns rapping over one beat. Each rapper uses clever rhymes and insults to make the crowd cheer and to win the contest. Freestyle battle raps vary from small gatherings in schools and neighborhoods to large publicized events. When he was young, Kendrick and his friends would have informal battles in the cafeteria and after school.

rap scene. He quickly became so good that no one wanted to rap with him.

All day Kendrick thought about rapping and music. He practiced at school and at home in his bedroom. He believes that without practice, his talent would have been wasted. By the time he was 16, Kendrick discovered that rapper 50 Cent gained fame by marketing the mixtapes he released. Kendrick started recording and releasing his music, too. In 2003, at the age of 16, he released his first mixtape. On the CD, Kendrick called himself K-Dot.

SIGNING WITH TOP DAWG ENTERTAINMENT

Kendrick's mixtape landed in the hands of Anthony "Top Dawg" Tiffith. Top Dawg was a music producer in the Compton area who had just started a small record

company called Top Dawg Entertainment. He liked Kendrick's mixtape so much that he called the teen into his studio.

While he pretended to ignore the young man, Top Dawg had Kendrick freestyle rap in his studio for two hours. In reality, Top Dawg was listening to Kendrick, and he loved what he heard. He thought that Kendrick had talent and signed him to a record contract.

BLACK HIPPY

Two weeks before Kendrick signed with Top Dawg Entertainment, Top Dawg signed Jay Rock, another teenage rapper from the Los Angeles area. Jay Rock also grew up in poverty and chose rap over gang involvement. Kendrick and

THE HISTORY OF MIXTAPES

When Kendrick was growing up, he and his dad often bought and listened to mixtapes. At that time, mixtapes were illegal cassettes or CDs of local rappers singing original verses over other people's beats. Later, beginning with the rapper 50 Cent, mixtapes became more like demo albums. Young, unsigned rappers would make mixtapes to show off their skills and distribute their music on the street.

Today, even famous rappers release mixtapes. These street albums often feature original songs and beats but are less polished and mainstream than studio releases. They often have many guest rappers and DJs. Today, mixtapes are often given away for free online.

Anthony "Top Dawg" Tiffith, *center*, met up with Kendrick, *left*, and rapper ScHoolboy Q at a 2016 basketball game in Los Angeles.

Jay Rock became friends and immediately started making music together.

Over time, two more young rappers joined the independent record label: Ab-Soul and ScHoolboy Q. In 2009, the group of four formed a rap super group, Black Hippy. The group began collaborating together and releasing songs. While Black Hippy has toured and remained active, they have never released a full album together.

Kendrick has said that in Black Hippy, each musician started in his own creative space and focused on what he did best. Then the group came together and picked the lines and beats they liked the most to create a song.

RUBBING SHOULDERS WITH GIANTS

"I was working on lyrics, writing, writing, writing on paper. And Kendrick goes in the booth with nothing. I asked him where's his paper? He'd written it all—the whole song—in his head in about five minutes. That's when I knew he was crazy. And a genius."[1]
—Jay Rock talking to Spin *magazine about rapping with Kendrick Lamar for the first time*

Still going by the rap name K-Dot, Kendrick released three more mixtapes between 2005 and 2009— *Training Day, No Sleep Til NYC,* and *C4.* He was slowly finding fans. He was also starting to get noticed by bigger rap stars in the industry. He was a featured rapper on songs by The Game and Lil Wayne. He and Jay Rock were also opening acts for The Game when he toured in 2006.

In 2009, Kendrick attended a HOT 97 radio event in New York City. At the event, up-and-coming rapper Charles Hamilton started a rap battle. A microphone was passed around the crowd and landed in Kendrick's hands.

He started rapping with skill and confidence. Although he was mostly unknown on the East Coast, everyone was impressed, including Hamilton. It was a sign of what was to come.

The Game's 2006 song "Hate It or Love It" was nominated for two Grammy Awards.

CHOOSING A DIFFERENT PATH

As Kendrick became better at rapping, he suddenly had a real dream and real goals. He thought about music all the time and focused on it completely. He spent less and less time getting in trouble with his friends. He stopped drinking and using drugs. He focused more on his religion.

At Centennial High School, Kendrick was a straight-A student who excelled in every subject. At the same time, his friends were suffering the consequences of being involved in crime and gangs. Many of them were receiving long prison sentences for their actions, while others were murdered during gang violence. Kendrick has said it was a gift from God for him to recognize that the gang lifestyle he had been born into was not the path for him.

BECOMING KENDRICK LAMAR, AGAIN

It was also around this time that Kendrick dropped his stage name, K-Dot, and began once again using his given name, Kendrick Lamar, when releasing music. He said in an interview that he wanted to use the name his mother had given him. In the song "Kendrick Lamar," he rapped about his choice

FAITH

Kendrick is a practicing Christian. He said that after a friend was shot and killed when he was 14, another friend's grandmother approached him and a group of friends in the parking lot of a grocery store. She asked if he had accepted God. "That was her being an angel for us," Kendrick told the New York Times.[2]

Kendrick's lifestyle reflects many traditional Christian morals regarding substance abuse and being faithful to one person. He rarely drinks or smokes. He does not spend much money on material things. He has been in a long-term relationship with his high school girlfriend for more than 10 years.

Kendrick considers himself a kind of preacher, and he knows that young fans see him as a role model. He takes that responsibility seriously. "My word will never be as strong as God's word," he said. "All I am is just a vessel, doing his work."[3]

Kendrick found his identity as a rapper.

LAMAR AND HIS MOM

Lamar's mother, Paula, has always been there for him, even when she showed him tough love. She also discussed tough issues with him as a child. She explained hard topics such as the Los Angeles riots, food stamps, welfare, and Section 8 housing.

The biggest lesson she taught Lamar was that he is ultimately in charge of change. He told *Rolling Stone*, "My moms always told me: 'How long you gonna play the victim?' I can say I'm mad and I hate everything, but nothing really changes until I change myself."[5] Lamar still keeps in close contact with his parents. He bought a home for them outside Los Angeles and visits often.

to use his given name: "No more K. Dot, my mother had named me Kendrick . . . Now finally I'm ready to tell the world who I are."[4]

After discovering his passion for rap and realizing who he was, Kendrick Lamar was finally ready to use his real name.

"He hasn't changed. He has a glow about him; he carries it with him. He's just a deep guy."[6]
—Ab-Soul, telling Spin magazine about his relationship with Kendrick through the Black Hippy rap group

THE NEW KING OF THE WEST COAST

Lamar had come in to his own by 2010. He had a record contract with an independent music company. He had produced four successful mixtapes. A few rap stars noticed him. More important, he had chosen music over street life and reclaimed his given name. He was ready to take the international rap world by storm. Time would tell if the rap world was ready for what he had to offer.

OVERLY DEDICATED

Lamar released his fifth mixtape, *Overly Dedicated*, on September 14, 2010. Unlike his other mixtapes, he recorded it under his birth name instead of his stage name. Another difference was that this mixtape took off, peaking at Number 72 on the Billboard Rap/

Lamar's career really began to take off in 2010.

Hip-Hop charts without the help of a major label or marketing efforts.

The record caught the attention of Dr. Dre, the same rapper Lamar had watched film a music video in Compton when he was a child on his father's shoulders. Dr. Dre saw the video for Lamar's song "Ignorance is Bliss" and was intrigued by the young rapper. He liked that Lamar used the same classic gangsta rap imagery and story lines as past rappers, but he had an elevated message that was not about glorifying life in Compton. Dr. Dre also watched some interviews with Lamar and liked the young rapper as a person.

Dr. Dre contacted Lamar and asked if he wanted to help him on his current album. Suddenly, Lamar found himself in a recording studio with two of the legends from his childhood—Snoop Dogg and Dr. Dre. The trio not only talked about music but also about life and how to be successful as a rapper. In addition, Dr. Dre and Lamar chatted about the possibility of Lamar joining Dre's Aftermath Entertainment company and becoming a major-label artist.

TOURING WITH TECH N9NE

Also during 2010, Lamar toured with Tech N9ne, a Kansas City, Missouri, rapper who founded his own independent label, Strange Music. Although Lamar was only acting as his friend Jay Rock's hype man during the opening act, he learned a lot on the tour about music, promotion, and his dreams for the future.

Lamar was impressed by the following that Tech N9ne had created on his own, through his smart business moves and hard work. Over the 48-day tour, they played 44 shows to crowds of thousands. The audience would sing along with every line of Tech N9ne's songs, and hundreds would come early for a chance to talk with the star. Lamar knew he wanted to follow the same path, either with a major record label or on his own.

XXL'S FRESHMAN CLASS ISSUE

Each year since 2007, hip-hop magazine *XXL* has released a list of ten up-and-coming rappers the editors believe are the future of the industry. The rappers must be new to the scene and cannot have a major label album release. Called the Freshman Class, these rappers are hotly debated before and after the publication of the magazine. They also receive national recognition for their work.

In the last ten years, *XXL* has picked some of the most talented rappers working today before they were famous, including Lupe Fiasco, Wale, Ace Hood, Kid Cudi, Wiz Khalifa, Future, Iggy Azalea, Chance the Rapper, and Action Bronson. In 2011, the year Lamar was selected, 11 rappers were chosen instead of ten: Kendrick Lamar, Meek Mill, Big K.R.I.T., Cyhi the Prynce, Lil Twist, Yelawolf, Fred the Godson, Mac Miller, YG, Lil B, and Diggy Simmons.

At the start of 2011, Lamar took another step toward fame and fortune. Along with ten other rising rappers, Lamar was chosen as part of *XXL* magazine's Freshman Class. At 23 years old, Lamar was on the cover of a national hip-hop magazine standing next to the most promising emcees in the world.

Lamar traveled to New York City to shoot the cover of the magazine with the other rappers and to have a roundtable interview with the other musicians. During the interview, Lamar got to know the other rising star rappers as he introduced himself to the world. Lamar had always been amazed and inspired by the Freshman Class rappers, and now he was one of them. He took time to enjoy the moment and meet the other artists, but he was also more motivated than ever to make music and have that music heard. He saw the magazine cover as an opportunity, so he worked even harder to achieve his dream.

> "I'm always going to stay true to the people that came up with me from the bottom, as far as my family and friends that wanted to see me get to a certain level of success. I'm supporting a lot of people now, just like they were supporting me when I had nothing."[1]
> –Kendrick Lamar in an interview for XXL's Freshman Class issue.

SECTION.80

Lamar released his first studio album through Top Dawg Entertainment in July 2011. The record, *Section.80*, was very ambitious. It was also different from other rap albums. It was a concept album that featured a cast of characters who lived in Compton during the late 1980s and 1990s. It discussed tough topics such as drug epidemics, poverty, and violence. It was not all about how great Lamar was. It was about the people in the neighborhood where he grew up.

The album entered the *Billboard* 200 at Number 113 and was certified gold by the Recording Industry Association of America (RIAA) in 2017 after selling 500,000 copies.[2] *Pitchfork Media* named the album Number 45 on its Best Albums of 2011 list, while *Complex* ranked it Number 7 on its top albums of the year list.

RIAA RECORDS

Artists receive gold certification from the Recording Industry Association of America when their song or album sells 500,000 copies and platinum certification when they sell one million copies. As of 2017, Lamar had earned four platinum certifications for songs or albums and five gold certifications.[3]

EARNING THE CROWN

A month after *Section.80* was released, Lamar performed at the Music Box in Hollywood in front of a packed crowd. Partway through the concert, The Game and Snoop Dogg surprised the audience with guest performances. Then they surprised Lamar by announcing that they were passing the torch to him. He was the new King of the West Coast.

Lamar wiped tears from his eyes as he was enveloped in a group hug by West Coast rap legends Snoop Dogg,

Snoop Dogg, *left*, was one of the first music giants to recognize Lamar's potential.

The Game, Warren G, and Kurupt. They were the rappers Lamar listened to when he was a kid, and now they looked up to him. They loved his music. He was realizing his dream.

"You ain't good at what you do. You great at what you do. If you got that torch, you better run with that torch."[4]

—Snoop Dogg, crowning Kendrick Lamar as the new King of the West Coast

MAJOR LABELS AND NEW MUSIC

By the beginning of 2012, Lamar was on the verge of national success. In just one year, he had gone on his first real tour with Tech N9ne, released his first studio album to critical acclaim, and appeared on the cover of hip-hop's hottest publication. In addition, the West Coast rappers whom he had idolized as a child had passed him the torch and told him it was his time to shine.

Always the thoughtful, quiet observer, Lamar knew it was his time to act. With his usual work ethic and deliberateness, he set to work on his next album. It would be his coming-of-age story. It would tell the complicated truth about Compton. By the end of 2012, it would be celebrated internationally.

Lamar accepts the award for Lyricist of the Year at the BET Hip-Hop Honors in 2012.

Black Hippy gathers for a 2013 event in Austin, Texas.

SIGNING A DEAL

Lamar had conflicting feelings about signing with a major record label. While on tour with Tech N9ne, Lamar was inspired by the Kansas City rapper's independent label and business skills. Lamar also felt very loyal to his independent label, Top Dawg Entertainment, which had supported him and promoted him since he was 16. When he was asked by *XXL* in 2011 if he wanted to sign with a major label, Lamar said he did not know.

But in March 2012, Lamar found a compromise. He and Top Dawg Entertainment signed a deal with a major label in which both labels would distribute Lamar's music together. They signed the deal with Aftermath Entertainment and Interscope records, the two music companies that Dr. Dre worked with. Black Hippy, Top Dawg's rap super group, signed a similar deal.

A GOOD KID IN A MAD CITY

Lamar wanted to write about Compton, as had many of the rappers he admired while growing up. But he wanted to capture the city like no one else had. He wanted to tell his own story of growing up in what he calls the "mad city." Top Dawg said that Lamar had the idea for his first major label album, *good kid,*

WHAT DOES *M.A.A.D CITY* STAND FOR?

Lamar often refers to his childhood self as being a "good kid in a mad city." He was trying his best to survive, but he was surrounded by poverty and gang violence. During a radio interview, he explained that the acronym "m.A.A.d" had two meanings. It stood for "my angry adolescence divided," which refers to the two worlds he lived in as a child—when he ran with a bad crowd and when he decided to stop. It also stood for "my angel's on angel dust."[1] This is a reference to a time Lamar smoked a drug when he did not know it was laced with PCP, a drug nicknamed "angel dust." After that experience, he decided he would no longer drink or do drugs.

CONSCIOUS RAP

Conscious rap artists think hard about the messages they send through their songs. They often focus on positive messages, such as nonviolence and equality. They also often focus on issues that are important to inner-city, mostly black neighborhoods, such as racism, discrimination, gang violence, police brutality, police shootings, and poverty. Conscious rappers want to create awareness, bust myths, and educate listeners. They care about social justice and politics.

Lamar is a conscious rapper. He often writes songs that spread awareness about growing up in urban poverty, being black, and being affected by violence. He also uses his songs to teach young listeners lessons about drug use, gang violence, police violence, and racism. Some of the most famous conscious rap artists and groups besides Lamar are Common, Talib Kweli, the Roots, Kanye West, Nas, and Lauryn Hill.

m.A.A.d city, years before he made it. Lamar was just waiting for the right time to tell his story.

The album is a first-person narrative. It takes place in 2004, and the characters are 17-year-old Lamar, his family, and his friends. The album captures the turbulent times when Lamar experimented with drugs and alcohol, ran with the wrong crowd, and broke the law. It is also about the good and bad aspects of the place he grew up.

In the conscious rap album, which is self-reflective and takes on social issues, Lamar discusses everything from getting his heart broken to committing a robbery to struggling with alcohol use. It has many of the themes of past rap albums but takes a more complex look at issues such as addiction, violence, racism, and poverty.

In an interview with the *Guardian*, Lamar said, "This album is a self-portrait. It's a piece to help me move on with my life and get past my former demons and better myself as a person. It was really a growing process so when I go back and listen to this, I can say, 'I did it.' Not just for me, but for people in Compton, too."[2]

Musically, Lamar showcases his raw ability to rap, from his quotable lines to his speed and razor-sharp delivery. His emotions emerge on each

"You don't hear no artists from Compton showing vulnerability. You always hear about the person pulling the trigger. You never hear about the one in front of it."[3]

–Kendrick Lamar

CONCEPT ALBUMS

A concept album is a record that has a larger meaning or theme. All of the songs on a concept album have something in common. In many cases, a concept album follows a story or narrative. In other cases, it is sung by a character the artist makes up. More rarely, a concept album could be about one issue or theme. Or it could be about a certain type of song or instrument. All of Lamar's major releases have been called concept albums, but *good kid, m.A.A.d city* is the most traditional one. The album is a narrative of Lamar's growing up in Compton. The songs include recurring characters, plots, and subplots.

track. With help from his producers and guest rappers, the album is musically diverse. It explores many subgenres of rap, from early 1990s gangsta rap sounds to more modern beats and rhythms. It also appealed to the masses, including fans of alternative music and indie rock.

ALBUM RECEPTION AND AWARDS

The *good kid, m.A.A.d city* album was almost universally acclaimed by music critics and appeared on many lists of the best albums of the year. Lamar was nominated for a *Billboard* Music Award and American Music Award. The record won BET's Best Album of the Year and Hip Hop Award, and Lamar also won BET's Lyricist of the Year and MVP of the Year.

The record debuted at Number 2 on the *Billboard* 200. It eventually sold more than one million albums and went platinum in August 2013.[4] Because of the album, Lamar got to perform for shows such as *Saturday Night Live, Late Night with David Letterman,* and *Late Night with Jimmy Fallon.* When the Grammy nominations were announced at the end of 2013, Lamar and *good kid, m.A.A.d city* secured seven nominations, including two of the biggest awards of the evening—Best New Artist and Best Album.

2014 GRAMMY AWARD NOMINATIONS

Lamar and his major label debut snagged seven Grammy nominations for 2014, including Best New Artist and Album of the Year. At the 56th Grammy Awards, Macklemore and Ryan Lewis won best new artist, while Daft Punk's Random Access Memories won Album of the Year. Here's the full list of Lamar's nominations:

- Best New Artist
- Album of the Year
- Best Rap Album
- Best Rap Performance: "Swimming Pools (Drank)"
- Best Rap Song: "F***in' Problems" (A$AP Rocky featuring Lamar, Drake, and 2 Chainz)
- Best Rap/Sung Collaboration: "Now or Never" (with Mary J. Blige)
- Best R&B Performance: "How Many Drinks?" (Miguel featuring Lamar)

Only one other artist, rap legend Jay-Z, received more nominations.

But on the night of the 2014 Grammy Awards, Lamar came up empty-handed. Macklemore, a rapper who was part of *XXL*'s 2012 Freshman Class, won many of the rap awards Lamar was nominated for. Macklemore texted Lamar and said that Lamar should have won. He posted the text online. Lamar congratulated his friend and was gracious about his losses.

At the awards show, Lamar performed his song "m.A.A.d city" live with the rock band Imagine Dragons. Dressed in all white, Lamar gave the performance of a lifetime as red smoke exploded around him. Some of the biggest stars in the business, including Taylor Swift, Queen Latifah, Steven Tyler, Lorde, and Robin Thicke, danced, smiled, and sang along. He proved he was at home performing with and for the greatest names in the industry.

THE COVER ART EXPLAINED

The cover of *good kid, m.A.A.d city* is a Polaroid picture from Lamar's childhood. He is a toddler, sitting with two of his uncles and his grandfather. On the wall behind them is a poster of Lamar and his father. On the table sits a bottle of beer and a bottle of milk. The eyes of everyone except Lamar are blacked out. Lamar explained in an interview with *Fuse* that the picture represents the album's music. It is a tale told only through his eyes and no one else's. It is a story about what it was like to be a kid growing up in a city filled with contradictions.

Chapter SEVEN

TO PIMP A BUTTERFLY

Lamar was in a hot, bright spotlight. In addition to his Grammy nominations, he was also named Rapper of the Year by *GQ* and appeared on the magazine's Men of the Year cover. In addition, rapper Kanye West asked Lamar to open for him on his first tour in five years, the Yeezus Tour, in the fall of 2013. Lamar and his producers told West that they needed to focus on recording new music, but West pressed them. He wanted an opening act that would be on par with his superstar performance. Finally, Lamar agreed to go, as long as he could bring a studio bus and record on the road. Many evenings, Lamar would perform before West and then spend the rest of the night recording and planning his next album.

Even while he was busy touring, Lamar worked furiously on his next album, hoping to top his previous success.

Lamar also performed in Barcelona, Spain, in 2014.

GAINING A NEW WORLDVIEW

Lamar traveled to South Africa in 2014. While visiting Durban, Johannesburg, and Cape Town, Lamar found inspiration for his next album. It would focus on the international experience of being black. It would include lots of history and many perspectives. It would be an album about social justice.

In an interview with the Recording Academy, Lamar said, "I felt like I belonged in Africa. I saw all the things that I wasn't taught. Probably one of the hardest things to do is put [together] a concept on how beautiful a place can be, and tell a person this while they're still in the ghettos of Compton. I wanted to put that experience in the music."[1]

One of his producers, Mark "Sounwave" Spears, said that when Lamar went to Africa, his mind clicked and the album started. Music mixer

Derek "MixedByAli" Ali said that Lamar took in everything he experienced in Africa like a sponge and incorporated it into the album, like "a million-piece puzzle."[2]

RELEASING THE ALBUM

On March 15, 2015, Lamar launched his third studio album, *To Pimp a Butterfly*. The 79-minute, 16-track project was different from his last album. It was multilayered, dense, loud, and at times angry. Instead of being about Lamar, it was focused on everyone. Instead of centering on Compton, it was about the whole world.

Over diverse music that included jazz, blues, soul, and funk, Lamar rapped about many important political issues in black history, including racial struggle, class, discrimination, and mass incarceration. There are

EXPERIMENTAL MUSIC

To Pimp a Butterfly was the first album by Lamar that was described as experimental. It mixes different types of sounds, including jazz, funk, hip-hop, and modern rap. In addition, the songs rarely followed traditional rap song structures. Experimental music pushes traditional boundaries, mixes genres, or adds new ingredients to songs, such as visuals or unusual sounds. All types of music can be experimental, from classical music to rock and roll. Experimental music can be challenging to listen to, but it can also break new ground and lead to wonderful new sounds and genres.

spoken word and a cappella sections, where there is singing but no background music. There are references to famous black activists and authors, as well as rap and hip-hop pioneers.

"The Blacker the Berry" was written within an hour after Lamar heard about the murder of Trayvon Martin. The song is charged with anger but turns toward self-reflection as Lamar grapples with racism, violence against black male teens, poverty, and some of the poor choices he made as a teen. The single was not only praised for its musical accomplishments but for its message.

To Pimp a Butterfly soared to the top of the

LAMAR ON *SATURDAY NIGHT LIVE*

Lamar first appearance on the television show *Saturday Night Live* on January 26, 2013. It happened after the release of *good kid, m.A.A.d city*. He performed "Swimming Pools (Drank)" and "Poetic Justice." During the first song, he rapped in front of a full band while bundled up in a coat and bathed in blue light. Later in the show, he returned in front of the band but in warmer light and short sleeves. He also made a short guest appearance in a comedy skit with host Adam Levine.

Lamar's second appearance on *Saturday Night Live* took place November 15, 2014. He performed two songs from *To Pimp a Butterfly*. First, he appeared in creepy black contact lenses to rap "i," again in front of a full band. He dedicated the song to his friends in prison. For Lamar's second song, singer-songwriter Chantal Kreviazuk played piano and sang, followed by Lamar's friend Jay Rock. Finally, Lamar emerged to rap his verse of "Pay for It."

Lamar wowed the crowd with a meaningful performance at the 2016 Grammys.

Billboard charts and sold the equivalent of one million copies within a year.[3] It was also almost universally praised by critics. The album appeared on end-of-the-year best album lists more than any other effort. Fifty-one

publications named it Best Album of the Year, including
Rolling Stone, *Pitchfork*, *Spin*, and *Complex*.

Lamar had been honest, shocking, and controversial in
To Pimp a Butterfly. He had made political statements that

other rappers often tiptoed around. And it had been an enormous success.

TRIUMPHANT RETURN TO THE GRAMMYS

Two years before, Lamar had stunned the audience with his Grammys performance, but he had not taken home any awards. Now he was back with his second major album and nominated for 11 Grammys, more than any other artist that year. It was the second most nominations in one night, behind Michael Jackson with 12 in 1984. Lamar also won more Grammys than any other performer that night: Best Rap Album, Best Rap Song ("Alright"),

COLLABORATING WITH TAYLOR SWIFT

Pop sensation Taylor Swift is a longtime fan of Lamar's. She often posts on social media about being a fan and talks about her respect for Lamar's music in interviews. She collaborated with Lamar on the remix of her hit song "Bad Blood" in 2015. The song became Swift's fourth Number 1 single from her album *1989* on the *Billboard* Hot 100. It was Lamar's first Number 1 single.

The song won Video of the Year and Best Collaboration at the 2015 MTV Video Music Awards. It also won Best Music Video at the 2016 Grammys. Lamar told *Billboard* about wanting to work with Swift: "She's passionate about her craft. When you put two people in the studio you have to have the same type of passion for the music in order for it to be right. It's not about the names; it's where we at sonically and creatively. . . . Can the music be great?"[4]

Best Rap Performance ("Alright"), Best Music Video ("Bad Blood"), and Best Rap/Sung Collaboration ("These Walls").

> "Each of his releases are more than a new chapter; they're an entirely different novel."[6]
> —*Julian Kimble*, Complex *magazine*

His performance, a medley of two of his new songs, was hailed as the performance of the night and one of the greatest Grammy acts ever. He began in prison clothes with his hands chained. His band was behind bars. Lamar spit his lyrics into the mic: "I'm African-American. . . . Your plan is to terminate my culture."[5] Then he transitioned to "Alright," his uplifting Black Lives Matter anthem. Chains dropped, Lamar and his performers danced around a bonfire, dressed in traditional African clothing. When the song ended, the crowd gave him a standing ovation.

DAMN.

According to his longtime producer Sounwave, Lamar did not wait a moment after *To Pimp a Butterfly* before beginning work on his next project. Lamar was ready to start something new and different, again. He rounded up his best producers and started recording songs for *DAMN.*

To Pimp a Butterfly was an experimental protest album that used free jazz and funk to tell stories and make political statements. *DAMN.* would be something else altogether. While *Butterfly* was about changing the world, Lamar said that *DAMN.* is about how you can't change the world until you change yourself.

Each of the songs, such as "PRIDE.," "HUMBLE.," "LUST.," and "LOVE.," focuses on a human emotion and how people should process that emotion. Because each track is about a different emotion, the album is very diverse. Each track has a different sound, theme, and approach.

DAMN. took Lamar in yet another direction musically.

UNTITLED. UNMASTERED.

In March 2016, Lamar released an eight-track compilation album called *Untitled. Unmastered.* It debuted at the top of the *Billboard 200*. The tracks were all demos recorded during the *To Pimp a Butterfly* period. Like that album, the songs on the compilation are dense, experimental songs about race, politics, social justice, and self-reflection. The album received positive reviews, despite the unpolished nature of the songs.

"At the end of the day [my success] is because people perceived me as a human being rather than an action figure that can't be touched."[1]

–*Kendrick Lamar*, Guardian interview, December 7, 2014

CAMEOS AND GUESTS

Lamar reached out to a large, diverse group of collaborators and producers to help him create the record that was forming in his mind. He and Sounwave asked many people to send him their music, while inviting others into the studio to work.

The final album contains many guest spots and cameos. After years of talking about collaborating, Lamar and U2's lead singer, Bono, worked on a track together. Bono sent Lamar a group of song ideas and vocals that Lamar turned into the song "XXX." Pop star Rihanna worked on one of the most popular singles from the album, "LOYALTY."

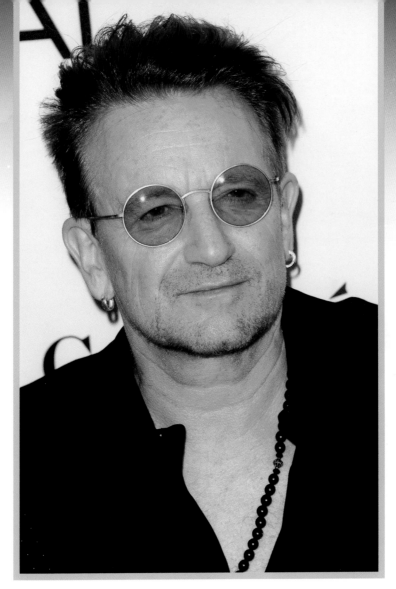

Bono fronts the Irish rock band U2.

Lamar also reached out to the Brooklyn pop artist Anna Wise about using some of her vocals on the record. She told *Rolling Stone* that she cried when she heard the final track, "PRIDE.," in which Lamar harmonizes with her emotional lyrics.[2]

A talented singer and songwriter, James Blake also plays piano.

After meeting several times, Lamar and the English singer-songwriter James Blake also agreed to collaborate. Lamar went to Blake's studio and saw one of his shows. One night he e-mailed Blake. Lamar asked if Blake could send music immediately. Blake sent some haunting piano chords, which were used on the song "ELEMENT."

Finally, R&B singer-songwriter Zacari Pacaldo was invited to Lamar's studio. Pacaldo did not know what to expect. When he played Lamar a new song called "Love," Lamar quieted down and said, "Yo, send that to me."[3] The final song, "LOVE.," features Pacaldo's beats and hooks mixed with Lamar's verses.

MAKING THE RECORD

By the time he started work on his fourth studio album, Lamar had more of a process in place for creating his music than ever before. Already known for his night owl tendencies and work ethic, he stayed in the studio 24 hours a day and asked that his producers do

LONGTIME LOVE

Lamar does not often talk about his romantic life, but he has revealed that he is engaged to his longtime girlfriend, Whitney Alford. He began dating Alford in high school, and they have been together for more than 12 years. Lamar confirmed they were engaged in 2015.

Lamar has said that Alford has been with him since day one and is one of the few people in his life with the power to call him out. He has also said that she is more than a girlfriend—she is his best friend. She is someone with whom he can share his fears.

At the 2016 Grammy Awards, Lamar thanked her for all she has done for him: "Whitney, I will always love you for supporting me and keeping me motivated to being the best person."[4]

the same. They slept in sleeping bags and accepted only short visits from friends and family.

Each song was deeply layered and closely examined and edited. Some songs, such as "ELEMENT.," went through 25 versions until Lamar was happy with every second of the piece. Unlike some rappers, Lamar is involved in every part of making his songs. He does not just rap. He creates the entire song in his head and then works with his producers to make his vision a reality.

When he thinks his album might be done, Lamar gets into a car with Sounwave, and they drive around the LA area and listen to it. If they do not get chills when the last song plays, they return to

DAMN.'S COVER ART

When Lamar released the cover art for *DAMN.* in April 2017, many fans were disappointed and confused by how it looked. The album features Lamar in a simple white t-shirt. He is standing in front of a red brick wall and is staring, unsmiling, at the camera. The album title is in a big, simple font. The Parental Advisory sticker is large and moved up from the corner.

Cover designer Vlad Sepetov, who also worked on the cover art for *To Pimp a Butterfly*, said that he went against what his design teachers taught him because he wanted to make something "loud and abrasive." He wanted to make "something that didn't fit the mold."[5]

Lamar, *right*, performs with Future at the 2017 BET Awards.

"Once he got his whole brainstorming thing down and we knew the direction we were going we locked down the studio for months. Never left. Literally sleeping bags in the studio."[6]

—*Producer Sounwave on the process of creating* DAMN.

the studio to work on it. Finally, after a few failed trips, the pair got chills, and Lamar's fourth studio album was done.

The next day, Lamar was back in the studio starting on his next project. He did not leave until four in the morning.

DAMN. debuted on April 14, 2017, at the top of the *Billboard* 200 and stayed there for weeks. By mid-2017, the album had sold 1.77 million album-equivalent units and was the most popular album of the year through the beginning of July.[7] Critics loved the album. Andy Kellman of *AllMusic* wrote, "It contains some of Lamar's best writing and performances, revealing his evolving complexity and versatility as a soul-baring lyricist and dynamic rapper."[8] In July, Lamar began his 17-date *DAMN*. tour across North America.

DUCKWORTH

"Duckworth" is the last song on *DAMN*. In this track, Lamar tells the story of how his dad, "Ducky," met Top Dawg, "Anthony," when Ducky was working at a KFC. The song states that Anthony had already robbed the fast-food store once, so Ducky decided to befriend him by giving Anthony free food whenever he came by. When Anthony once again robbed the KFC, he chose not to shoot Ducky. The song appreciates how small good acts can change the course of a person's life, as Lamar raps, "Because if Anthony killed Ducky, Top Dawg could be servin' life / While I grew up without a father and die in a gunfight."[9] Years later, Top Dawg would help make Lamar's career as a rapper.

GROWING INTO THE FUTURE

In the music video for "King Kunta," Lamar and his posse celebrate throughout the city of Compton. As Lamar raps about the issues most important to him and his community, he visits the most formative locations of his youth. At one point, the video shows the Compton Swap Meet. This is the place where Kendrick's father took him to buy mixtapes as a child. It is also the very place he saw Dr. Dre and Tupac Shakur film the rap video for "California Love" on the day he was first inspired to rap.

So much had happened since the day Kenny put his son on his shoulders to see his rap mentors make history. Lamar worked hard in school, devoted all of his energy to music, and made it to the top based on his raw talent and effort. He has become a role model for countless kids, not only in Compton, but around the globe.

By September 2017, Lamar had five of the top 50 most-streamed songs of the year.

Compton mayor Aja Brown presents Lamar with the key to the city.

"When Tupac was here and I saw him as a 9-year-old, I think that was the birth of what I'm doing today. From the moment that he passed I knew the things he was saying would eventually be carried on through someone else. But I was too young to know that I would be the one doing it."[1]

–Kendrick Lamar

THE KEY TO THE CITY

On February 13, 2016, Compton mayor Aja Brown presented Lamar with the symbolic key to the city during a moving ceremony. She told Lamar that he was an amazing performer who raised consciousness with his music. She added, "His

message challenges the status quo and motivates listeners to rethink our society's institutions."[2]

When accepting the key, Lamar talked about his childhood and how the spirit of Compton gave him strength. He also said that no matter where his career takes him, he would always

"He represents Compton with great pride and I am honored to present him with the Key to the City, which symbolizes our deep appreciation for his philanthropic work and commitment to our community. Mr. Lamar's achievements further Compton's legacy of ingenuity and excellence."[3]

—Compton mayor Aja Brown, giving Lamar the key to the city

return to Compton and do right by it. The crowd, listening to his speech, chanted his inspiring lyrics: "We gon' be alright!"[4]

KING KENDRICK

By 2017, Lamar was widely considered the most critically acclaimed rapper in the world and one of the most influential artists creating music. He had three RIAA platinum albums and three albums that rose to the top spot on the *Billboard* 200.[5] He had won seven Grammy Awards and was named among the 100 most influential people in the world by *Time* magazine in 2016.

Perhaps more important, he has positively affected his listeners. Not only does he make exceptional experimental rap, he also connects with fans who have experienced poverty, racism, violence, police brutality, addiction, and incarceration. More than that, his narrative, self-reflective lyrics connect with anyone who has been on

SOCIAL MEDIA

Unlike many stars in the music business, Lamar mostly shies away from social media. When he does use Twitter or Instagram, it is to post big music news or share other music he likes. He does not often interact with others, argue, or post his opinions. Just as he was when he was a child, he is a quiet observer more than a social talker. He uses his songs to share his thoughts.

He also does not want to get caught up in praise or distracted from his current projects. He told Erykah Badu in *Interview* magazine: "I try my best to stay away from social media as much as possible. When you go on your Twitter or look down your timeline and it's all great positivity, I love that. But at the same time, it can really divert you from what your purpose is or what you're trying to do."[6]

a difficult journey, doubted themselves, or strived to accomplish a big dream.

FOREGOING THE BLING

Through his rise to fame, Lamar never took to the lavish lifestyle of many of the rappers who came before him. Even today, despite making millions of dollars each year for his work, he does not have extravagant jewelry or a garage full of fancy cars.

His largest purchase has been a home for his parents in the suburbs of East Los Angeles. Instead of in a mansion, he lives with his fiancée, Whitney Alford, in a three-level condo not far from the Compton neighborhood where he grew up. He admits he does

not like to throw money around at clubs or spend it on material goods. He would rather work in the studio.

Lamar has said that he used to think that money was something that would make him happy, but he has discovered that he has felt better being able to help his parents, his family, and the people who have supported him since the beginning. He says he would not know what to do in a mansion.

WHAT'S NEXT?

Lamar is always evolving. He has never been happy making the same kind of record twice, even if the record is a great one. During his career, he has made an album about his past, a protest record, and a record about his inner struggles. Whatever he is working on now, the past tells us it will be dense, complex, introspective, and sharp. It will also likely change the way his listeners look at the world and listen to music.

As for Lamar himself, he told Erykah Badu in an interview that he is simply trying to live in the moment and be himself—just as he has always done.

MEDITATION

Lamar likes to meditate for 30 minutes every day or every other day. He sits back, closes his eyes, and thinks about the moment he is in. He explains that with his schedule, he is either working in the studio or on tour for months at a time. With his whirlwind schedule and his quick rise to fame, time can slip by, and it is easy to forget to enjoy the moment. For this reason, he has also kept journals in the past.

Lamar enjoys giving back, whether through his music or through his charity work.

TIMELINE

1987

On June 17, Kendrick Lamar Duckworth is born in Compton, California.

1995

Lamar watches Dr. Dre and Tupac film their music video for "California Love."

2003

Lamar releases his first mixtape under the rap name K-Dot.

2004

Lamar signs his first record deal, with Top Dawg Entertainment.

2009

Lamar drops his rap name K-Dot and begins to use his real name; Lamar joins Black Hippy, a rap super group, with Jay Rock, Ab-Soul, and ScHoolboy Q.

2011

Lamar releases his first official studio album, *Section.80*; during a Los Angeles concert, Lamar is called the "New King of the West Coast" by rap legends Dr. Dre, The Game, and Snoop Dogg.

2012

Lamar signs with Aftermath Entertainment and Interscope Records; Lamar drops his major label debut, *good kid, m.A.A.d city*.

2013

Lamar goes on the Yeezus Tour, opening for Kanye West.

2015

Lamar's second major album, *To Pimp a Butterfly*, is released; Black Lives Matter protesters begin to chant his song "Alright" at marches; Lamar wins his first two Grammy Awards, for Best Rap Song and Best Rap Performance ("i").

2016

Lamar wins five Grammys for his work related to his *To Pimp a Butterfly* album and for his work with Taylor Swift on "Bad Blood."

2017

Lamar's third major album, *DAMN.*, is released; he embarks on his 17-date *DAMN.* tour across North America.

FULL NAME
Kendrick Lamar Duckworth

DATE OF BIRTH
June 17, 1987

PLACE OF BIRTH
Compton, California

PARENTS
Kenny Duckworth and Paula Oliver

EDUCATION
Centennial High School in Compton, California

FIANCÉE
Whitney Alford

CAREER HIGHLIGHTS
Kendrick Lamar has had four songs or albums go platinum and five songs or albums go gold. He has received seven Grammy Awards and 22 Grammy nominations as of 2017. In addition, he has won five BET Awards and received Compton's key to the city.

ALBUMS
Section.80 (2011); *good kid, m.A.A.d city* (2012); *To Pimp a Butterfly* (2015); *DAMN.* (2017)

CONTRIBUTION TO HIP-HOP

Kendrick Lamar has elevated West Coast rap far beyond its worst aspects: being self-centered, putting down women, and glorifying gang life. Instead, he uses rap to convey meaningful stories, build understanding, and spread messages of social justice. Musically, he has broken new ground in rap when it comes to developing new sounds, experimenting with blending genres, and developing concept albums.

CONFLICTS

Born into poverty and surrounded by gang activity and violence, Kendrick Lamar found himself getting involved in drugs, alcohol, and crime during his early teens. But he found meaning in music and overcame hardship to become a talented rapper who helps others through his music, his example, and his charity.

QUOTE

"At the end of the day [my success] is because people perceived me as a human being rather than an action figure that can't be touched."

—*Kendrick Lamar*

BAR

A measure of music in rap songs, 16 bars make up a verse.

COLLABORATE

To work together with someone else on a project.

FUNK

A danceable genre of music that combines soul, jazz, and blues.

GENRE

A category of music with similarities in sound, form, style, or subject matter.

INDEPENDENT RECORD LABEL

A recording company that does not receive funding from a major, commercial recording company.

INTROVERT

A shy, reflective person who gets energy from being alone.

JAZZ

A genre of music developed by African Americans that is characterized by rhythm and improvisation. Brass, woodwind, and percussion instruments are associated with the genre.

NARRATIVE

A story or account of events.

NOMINATE

To choose or suggest someone for a special honor or award.

POLICE BRUTALITY

The use of excessive and unlawful force on a citizen by a police officer.

PRODUCER

Someone who organizes projects, makes suggestions, mixes sounds, and coaches the artist in the studio.

RACISM

Discrimination or prejudice against a specific race or cultural background.

RECORD CONTRACT

A legal agreement between an artist and recording company that promotes and sells music.

REMIX

A different version of a song that might have guest appearances or a new beat.

SECTION 8 HOUSING

Government-assisted rental housing for low-income families.

SINGLE

A standalone song that is distributed to radio stations and the media.

SOCIAL JUSTICE

The equal distribution of opportunities and resources; the view that all people should have equal rights.

SELECTED BIBLIOGRAPHY

Collins, Hattie. "Kendrick Lamar: The Rise of a Good Kid Rapper in a Mad City." *Guardian*. Guardian News and Media Limited. 7 Dec. 2012. Web. 25 Aug. 2017.

Eells, John. "The Trials of Kendrick Lamar." *Rolling Stone*. Rolling Stone. 22 June 2015. Web. 25 Aug. 2017.

Goodman, Lizzie. "Kendrick Lamar: Hip Hop's Newest Old School Star." *New York Times*. New York Times. 25 June 2014. Web. 25 Aug. 2017.

Hopper, Jessica. "Kendrick Lamar Is Not Your Average Everyday Rap Savior." *Spin*. Spin. 9 Oct. 2012. Web. 25 Aug. 2017.

FURTHER READINGS

Higgins, Dalton. *Hip Hop World*. Berkeley, CA: Groundwork, 2009. Print.

Hoblin, Paul. *Jay-Z: Hip-Hop Mogul*. Minneapolis: Abdo, 2012. Print.

Klepeis, Alicia Z. *Kanye West: Music Industry Influencer*. Minneapolis: Abdo, 2018. Print.

ONLINE RESOURCES

Booklinks
NONFICTION NETWORK
FREE! ONLINE NONFICTION RESOURCES

To learn more about Kendrick Lamar, visit **abdobooklinks.com**. These links are routinely monitored and updated to provide the most current information available.

MORE INFORMATION

For more information on this subject, contact or visit the following organizations:

CITY OF COMPTON
comptoncity.org
205 S. Willowbrook Ave.
Compton, CA 90220
310-605-5500

Learn more about the history of the city where Kendrick Lamar and many other notable rap stars were born. Also plan your visit by reading about local landmarks, museums, parks, and events.

GRAMMY MUSEUM
grammymuseum.org
800 W. Olympic Blvd., Ste. A245
Los Angeles, CA 90015
213-765-6800

Visit this interactive, educational museum to learn all about the past winners of Grammy Awards as well as the history of American music, including rap and hip-hop.

INTERSCOPE RECORDS
interscope.com
2220 Colorado Ave.
Santa Monica, CA 90404
310-865-1000

Get the latest news and videos from Interscope's musical artists or write a letter to Kendrick Lamar or other rap and hip-hop artists.

SOURCE NOTES

CHAPTER 1. THE ANTHEM OF A GENERATION

1. Jamilah King. "The Improbable Story of How Kendrick Lamar's 'Alright' Became a Protest Anthem." *Mic*. Mic Network, 11 Feb. 2016. Web. 2 Oct. 2017.

2. Aisha Harris. "Has Kendrick Lamar Recorded the New Black National Anthem?" *Slate*. The Slate Group, 3 Aug. 2015. Web. 2 Oct. 2017.

3. *XXL* Staff. "Kendrick Lamar on TDE, His 'Control' Verse and Fame From *XXL*'s Oct/Nov Cover Story." *XXL*. XXL Network, 23 Oct. 2013. Web. 2 Oct. 2017.

CHAPTER 2. COMING UP IN COMPTON

1. Carman Tse. "How Compton Became the Violent City of 'Straight Outta Compton.'" *Laist*. Gothamist LLC, 14 Aug. 2015. Web. 2 Oct. 2017.

2. John Eells. "The Trials of Kendrick Lamar." *Rolling Stone*. Rolling Stone, 22 June 2015. Web. 2 Oct. 2017.

3. Ross Scarano. "Kendrick Lamar's Guide to L.A." *Complex*. Complex Media Inc., 26 Oct. 2012. Web. 2 Oct. 2017.

4. John Eells. "The Trials of Kendrick Lamar." *Rolling Stone*. Rolling Stone, 22 June 2015. Web. 2 Oct. 2017.

CHAPTER 3. DISCOVERING POETRY AND RAP

1. "Resources." *National Stuttering Association*. Westutter.org, n.d. Web. 2 Oct. 2017.

2. John Eells. "The Trials of Kendrick Lamar." *Rolling Stone*. Rolling Stone, 22 June 2015. Web. 2 Oct. 2017.

3. Adam Bradley. "Why Is Pop Music the People's Poetry? That's What They Like." *Los Angeles Times*. Los Angeles Times, 7 May 2017. Web. 2 Oct. 2017.

4. Jessica Hopper. "Kendrick Lamar: Not Your Average Everyday Rap Savior." *Spin*. Billboard-Hollywood Reporter Media Group, 9 Oct. 2012. Web. 2 Oct. 2017.

5. Hattie Collins. "Kendrick Lamar: The Rise of a Good Kid Rapper in a Mad City." *Guardian*. Guardian News and Media Limited, 12 Dec. 2012. Web. 2 Oct. 2017.

6. Kate. "Kendrick Lamar Talks His Father, J. Cole Production and Hiiipower." *Rapdose*. Rapdose.com, 2 July 2011. Web. 2 Oct. 2017.

7. Jessica Hopper. "Kendrick Lamar: Not Your Average Everyday Rap Savior." *Spin*. Billboard-Hollywood Reporter Media Group, 9 Oct. 2012. Web. 2 Oct. 2017.

8. John Eells. "The Trials of Kendrick Lamar." *Rolling Stone*. Rolling Stone, 22 June 2015. Web. 2 Oct. 2017.

CHAPTER 4. MAKING MIXTAPES AND MORE

1. Jessica Hopper. "Kendrick Lamar: Not Your Average Everyday Rap Savior." *Spin*. Billboard-Hollywood Reporter Media Group, 9 Oct. 2012. Web. 2 Oct. 2017.

2. Joe Coscarelli. "Kendrick Lamar on His New Album and the Weight of Clarity." *New York Times*. New York Times, 16 March 2015. Web. 2 Oct. 2017.

3. Ibid.

4. Kendrick Lamar. "Compton State of Mind." *Genius*. Genius Media Group, n.d. Web. 2 Oct. 2017.

5. John Eells. "The Trials of Kendrick Lamar." *Rolling Stone*. Rolling Stone, 22 June 2015. Web. 2 Oct. 2017.

6. Jessica Hopper. "Kendrick Lamar: Not Your Average Everyday Rap Savior." *Spin*. Billboard-Hollywood Reporter Media Group, 9 Oct. 2012. Web. 2 Oct. 2017.

CHAPTER 5. THE NEW KING OF THE WEST COAST

1. "Introducing *XXL* Freshman Kendrick Lamar." *XXL*. XXL Network, Web. 2 Oct. 2017.

2. "Gold & Platinum." *RIAA*. RIAA, Web. 2 Oct. 2017.

3. Ibid.

4. Alex Gale. "20 Legendary Hip Hop Concert Moments." *Complex*. Complex Media, 24 May 2013. Web. 2 Oct. 2017.

CHAPTER 6. MAJOR LABELS AND NEW MUSIC

1. Steven Horowitz. "Kendrick Lamar Explains Meaning Of 'good kid, m.A.A.d city' Title, Reveals T.I. Collaboration." *HipHopDX*. HipHopDx, 19 Oct. 2012. Web. 2 Oct. 2017.

2. Hattie Collins. "Kendrick Lamar: The Rise of a Good Kid Rapper in a Mad City." *Guardian*. Guardian News and Media Limited, 12 Dec. 2012. Web. 2 Oct. 2017.

3. Ibid.

4. "Gold & Platinum." *RIAA*. RIAA, n.d. Web. 2 Oct. 2017.

CONTINUED

CHAPTER 7. *TO PIMP A BUTTERFLY*

1. Andreas Hale. "'To Pimp a Butterfly': Kendrick Lamar Shares History." *Recording Academy Grammy Awards*. Recording Academy, 15 May 2017. Web. 2 Oct. 2017.

2. Ibid.

3. "Gold & Platinum." *RIAA*. RIAA, Web. 2 Oct. 2017.

4. Andreas Hale. "'To Pimp a Butterfly': Kendrick Lamar Shares History." *Recording Academy Grammy Awards*. Recording Academy, 15 May 2017. Web. 2 Oct. 2017.

5. Melonyce McAffee. "How Kendrick Lamar's Fiery Performance Won Grammy Night." *CNN*. Cable News Network, 18 Feb. 2016. Web. 2 Oct. 2017.

6. John Eells. "The Trials of Kendrick Lamar." *Rolling Stone*. Rolling Stone, 22 June 2015. Web. 2 Oct. 2017.

CHAPTER 8. *DAMN.*

1. Hattie Collins. "Kendrick Lamar: The Rise of a Good Kid Rapper in a Mad City." *Guardian*. Guardian News and Media Limited, 12 Dec. 2012. Web. 2 Oct. 2017.

2. David Browne. "Kendrick Lamar's '*DAMN.*': Inside the Making of the Number One LP." *Rolling Stone*. Rolling Stone, 1 May 2017. Web. 2 Oct. 2017.

3. Ibid.

4. "Kendrick Lamar Wins Best Rap Album at Grammys" *Rap-Up*. Rap-Up.com, 15 Feb. 2016. Web. 2 Oct. 2017.

5. Cherise Johnson. "Kendrick Lamar's '*DAMN.*' Graphic Designer Defends Album Artwork." *HipHopDX*. HipHopDX, 12 Apr. 2017. Web. 2 Oct. 2017.

6. Dan Hyman. "Why Kendrick Lamar and Sounwave Camped Out in Sleeping Bags to Make *DAMN.*" *GQ*. Condé Nast, 22 Apr. 2017. Web. 2 Oct. 2017.

7. Keith Caulfield. "Kendrick Lamar's '*DAMN.*' & Ed Sheeran's 'Shape of You' Lead Nielsen Music's Mid-Year 2017 Charts." *Billboard*. Billboard, 5 July 2017. Web. 2 Oct. 2017.

8. Andy Kellman. "Kendrick Lamar: *DAMN.*" *AllMusic*. AllMusic, n.d. Web. 2 Oct. 2017.

9. Kendrick Lamar. "Duckworth." *Genius*. Genius Media Group, n.d. Web. 23 Oct. 2017.

CHAPTER 9. GROWING INTO THE FUTURE

1. Andreas Hale. "To Pimp a Butterfly': Kendrick Lamar Shares History." *Recording Academy Grammy Awards*. Recording Academy, 15 May 2017. Web. 2 Oct. 2017.

2. Jackson McHenry. "Kendrick Lamar Receives the Key to the City of Compton." *Vulture*. New York Media, 14 Feb. 2016. Web. 2 Oct. 2017.

3. Ibid.

4. Ibid.

5. "Kendrick Lamar." *Billboard*. Billboard-Hollywood Reporter Media Group, n.d. Web. 2 Oct. 2017.

6. Erykah Badu. "Kendrick Lamar." *Interview*. Interview, 8 May, 2013. Web. 2 Oct. 2017.

Sarah Aswell is a writer who lives in Missoula, Montana, with her husband, Ben, and their two daughters, Willa and Josephine. She attended Grinnell College and received her master of fine arts degree in Creative Writing from the University of Montana. Her favorite rappers, besides Kendrick Lamar, include Missy Elliott, Jay-Z, Kanye West, Big Boi, and Rick Ross.